Tow Trucks

Kate Riggs

CREATIVE EDUCATION • CREATIVE PAPERBACKS

seedlings

Published by Creative Education and Creative Paperbacks
P.O. Box 227, Mankato, Minnesota 56002
Creative Education and Creative Paperbacks
are imprints of The Creative Company
www.thecreativecompany.us

Design by Ellen Huber; production by Joe Kahnke
Art direction by Rita Marshall
Printed in the United States of America

Photographs by Affordable Towing of Mankato, Minnesota;
Alamy (Aurora Photos, B Christopher, INSADCO Photography);
Corbis (Richard Hamilton Smith); Dreamstime (Robert Crum,
Robwilson39, Seagames50, Edwin Verin); iStockphoto (abalcazar,
comptine, DNY59, kozmoat98, leezsnow, njpPhoto, Terry Wilson);
Shutterstock (Baloncici, Vereshchagin Dmitry, alexander briel
perez, Taina Sohlman, ThamKC)

Library of Congress Cataloging-in-Publication Data
Riggs, Kate.
Tow trucks / Kate Riggs.
p. cm. — (Seedlings)
Includes bibliographical references and index.
Summary: A kindergarten-level introduction to tow trucks,
covering their purpose, where they are found, their drivers,
and such defining features as their booms and winches.
ISBN 978-1-60818-794-2 (hardcover)
ISBN 978-1-62832-390-0 (pbk)
ISBN 978-1-56660-824-4 (eBook)
This title has been submitted for
CIP processing under LCCN 2016937124.

CCSS: RI.K.1, 2, 3, 4, 5, 6, 7;
RI.1.1, 2, 3, 4, 5, 6, 7; RF.K.1, 3; RF.1.1

First Edition HC 9 8 7 6 5 4 3 2 1
First Edition PBK 9 8 7 6 5 4 3 2 1

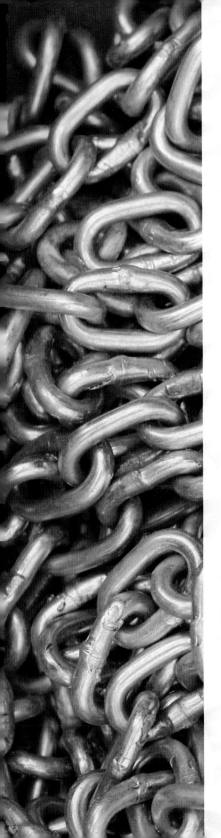

TABLE OF CONTENTS

Hello,
tow trucks!

Tow trucks help other vehicles.

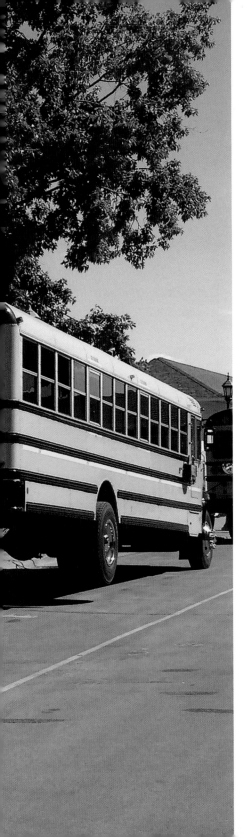

They take broken ones to get fixed. They move them to other places.

Many tow trucks have a boom. On the boom is a winch.

This pulls or lifts heavy things.

Some tow trucks lift cars by their wheels. A metal yoke fits under the wheels.

The driver sits inside a tow truck. He gets out to hook up a car to his truck.

A tow truck can have a boom and a wheel-lift. Or it can have a flatbed. The bed lowers to put a vehicle on.

Tow trucks find vehicles in trouble. They help at accidents.

They take cars out of ditches.

Goodbye,
tow trucks!

Picture a Tow Truck

cab

bumper

wheel

light bar

boom

yoke

tool box

Words to Know

boom: a moveable arm

flatbed: a flat area that carries loads

yoke: a crossbar that fits under the wheels of a car to lift it

Read More

Manolis, Kay. *Tow Trucks.*
Minneapolis: Bellwether Media, 2009.

Nixon, James. *Trucks.*
Mankato, Minn.: Amicus, 2011.

Websites

Tow Trucks Craft
http://www.thebestkidsbooksite.com/craftdetails3
.cfm?CraftID=411
Make your own tow truck out of paper and other materials.

Trucks Coloring Pages
http://www.coloring.ws/trucks.htm
Print out pictures of tow trucks and other trucks to color.

Note: Every effort has been made to ensure that the websites listed above are suitable for children, that they have educational value, and that they contain no inappropriate material. However, because of the nature of the Internet, it is impossible to guarantee that these sites will remain active indefinitely or that their contents will not be altered.

23

Index